The
Windowless Soul

The
Windowless Soul
Poetic expression of emotion

Michael T. Mushonga

For more information,
contact: miketatenda@hotmail.com

First paperback edition 2023

978-1-80541-091-1 (paperback)
978-1-80541-092-8 (ebook)

Dedicated to

Evangelista Mushonga

Your motherly love is evidence that God exists

Contents

Times and Seasons

Sound

The sound of my fear is a song uncomposed.
I'm gone.
Sons and Daughters become their father and mothers,
Old, grey, wrinkled, poetic and full of life.
Tomorrow,
A vision today cannot fathom.
My destination?
A location unknown but reached in blind night.

Memories of the lyrics that dance with sound.
Four years old,
Walking slowly towards the voice of a proud father,
Dancing to the sound of happiness and life,
Sleeping in the arms of a loving mother,
And four years later her arms were the only thing left.

Life, a song ending before a harmonic chorus.

Time

Anxiously waiting for a single moment,
Floating in a cloud of hope and expectation,
Constantly thinking on extraordinary first impressions,
Hellos are easier than goodbyes they preached,
My soul is too old for introductions,
Why can't today be our last connection?
Why can't today be the first of forever?
Two opposites attract energy Miss,
The sun has met his moon.
Light up my star-covered night as I brighten up your day.
A great painter takes time to master the brush,
Let's paint an amazing picture titled 'Till death do us part'.

What is time?
What is now?
What is love?

Time accounts for every second I want to make your
body tremble in heaven-sent satisfaction,
Now is the first moment of a happiness you'll wrap
yourself around for a lifetime in my arms,
Love isn't defined by words but the spontaneous
seconds.
I'll show you how stars twinkle in your eyes when you're
breathless from immense gratification of my love for
you.

Thought

The candle-lit room on hell street,
So cold is the irony,
So bold are the imperfect,
Nightmares walk my reality,
Dreams are the subtle hugs my grandmother gave me,
Will she be still there when I'm old and grey?
Will the night twinkle with the stars of life?
Will death be quick and painless?

Drunk

A small time frame,
A mere fragment of existence,
When problems suddenly disappear.
Move your feet, left and right,
Let beautiful music control
your body like a puppet master,
Dance, dance, stagger and dance.
You deserve your sanity.

Full Moon

Listen to the sound of my soul,
Filled by a big void the masses call emptiness.
Each breath expands depth,
Brewed an attachment to it.
When dawn breaks,
Our bond shares an intimate hand clasp.
When night haunts the world,
Our bond turns gruesome.
Eyes tend to carry weight,
Heart rate quickens,
Mental disorders come out to dance,
In the moment of being alone
One mirrors his true self.

Stars

How infinite are the stars,
How are they birthed in darkness,
Caged by coldness and blank light years,
Individually watching over us.
Our guardians? Our gods?
The unreachable heavens in the sky,
Sing me a soundless song,
The great gospel of space.
Did my past see what I see,
Or was it a dream gone without a trace?

The Sunflower

Covered in summer's sunshine,
The she-loves-me rose petal left,
A slow dance on our 50th wedding anniversary.
If death was an option
I'd dare choose an endless life with you,
The song of youth,
Her chorus ever more mesmerising,
The sweet melody of love,
How we dance in tune,
Hold my hand Sunflower,
We are bound for infinity.

Age

Butterflies are born from caterpillars,
You crawl, walk and run towards the end,
A song with an off-beat chorus,
How bad are the lessons learnt?
How memorable will the moments be?

1.

Filled with love and ignorance,
The world,
A blinding rainbow with lotus flowers falling like rain on
the sad baby's cheeks.
How infinite are the possibilities of overzealous
destinies,
Yet mother rests you on her beating heart and you
instantly decide you love her like a loyal military officer
before his commander,
And the idea of tomorrow is a promise yet to be broken.

13.

Reeking of puberty and ignorance,
The world,
A complicated equation with an outside-of-the-formula
answer,
Feelings and emotions choke you as they stand there
silently betting on your end.
In this moment in time your first lessons begin.

18.

Heartbroken and alone,
The combination of youth,
Misguided and trusts less,
How poetic is age,
Truly wine doesn't taste better but bitter.

23.

Sanity is the concept of an unimaginable reality,
Responsibilities spawn like pimples I skipped during
puberty,
My purpose is a dream I wake up forgetting.
Will this university experience be the pinnacle of my
maturity?

Writer's Block

To the gods of song I prostate in passion,
I ask for my pen to return in fashion,
For my ink runs dry on the canvas of flowery hymns,
Like the Venice art on the display of collected brims.

I dance in frustration to the beat of agony,
I lyricize my anguish to the thoughts of writer's block
fallacy,
Chastity I keep my voice in thoughts,
For the breaking of silence shall be judged in Zeus's
courts.

Here my lamentations and dry thy leaking eyes,
Here my thoughts and be as appealing as a lover's
thighs,
Here ends writer's block hellos and goodbyes.

Austerity

Awake from the aftermath of austerity,
Dance on the pieces of dreams scattered on the floor of
humanity,
Reminisce on the bullets that missed your body,
For in each passing moment life is lived till the rags are
faded glory.
Where do I stand in the lyrical existence of birth and
creation?
Which stone will foundation my home before death's
invasion?
The howling wolf is crying out to the gods of mankind,
He calls out for his soul as empty I-love-you's he tends
to find,
I must be out of my mind.
The words I leave behind are my thoughts I tried to tell
you all the time,
I was a man who thought the universe was the soul of
creation,

Is existentialism at war with the divine was my subject of
dissertation.
As I graduate to the afterlife,
I hope my experience on earth will be a memory
remembrance cannot fathom.

Damaged

Crucify yourself under the night sky,
Call to the heavens and listen to silence,
The raven flies from a distance,
Look into my eyes and feel the emptiness,
Nails plunged into my flesh,
My horrific screams fill the night,
Nails, an excuse for me to shed a tear,
Mental illness the most underrated torturer,
Lost in a galaxy scientists can't visit in a therapy session.

The raven flies closer and closer,
Lands on my shoulder,
Looks into the darkness in my eyes and whispers,
"Your time is finally up."

Mr Ethics

I'm a scholar of ethics
Subconsciously I ask, why am I teaching?
I detest measures taken drastic,
Why is society so deceiving?
Election campaigns, a podium for the best outspoken
falsifier,
Morality a sip that's tipped to get manipulative powerful
men vilified,
Their motto screams to belittle the young activists to
sleep minus the pacifier,
Pacifists are seen as unethical as societies' past shows
how the African heritage died.
I cried, as a young man in a man's world,
Tears invisible before my masculinity is toxified.
I cried, as a young African away from the motherland in
a faraway world,
Tears invisible before my outcries for injustices are a
mere ice-cube to be liquefied.
Consciously you're afraid of the world,
Subconsciously you're just afraid of yourself.

What's the outcome for trying to change the world
without viable solutions?
Humanity has turned itself into its own pollution,
Malnutrition on UNICEF ads is a picture away from a
million retweets,
But a million dollars away for the world to rethink.
Please let that sink.
In this now I say let me get high from the weeds of my
uprooted ancestors,
The fake bilateral agreements sunk our ships and
enriched your harbours,
Your fathers sardined us and deemed us as special
labourers,
I understand the beauty of conservatism if its
functionality is to protect your reservation.

Let me get down from this podium before my random
thoughts drunken those listening.

Flying Colours

Take me to Valhalla,
The hall of my forefathers,
The place where souls infinitely dance.

Take me to heaven,
The place where my mother waits,
The happiness I'm yet to feel as wings clasp her child.

Memories are the mind's tattoo,
A lifetime of melting ink carved on volcanic dementia,
How forgetful is the broken soul?

Rainbow,
The name you once gave a stranger called life,
The end isn't gold, it's pain for the colours that still show,
Will my knees ache from calling to the sky.
Mother!
The weight of my heart sinking is choking,
Will my call be answered?

In this midst of thought,
The crimson lines paint the sky,
The flying colours that float in the heavens.

Is this it?
Are you watching down on me from your mute
pedestal?

The flying colours that bond you and I.

Machines

The unmoved eyes stuck on his face,
His glare,
Empty, like the darkness in the deep oceans,
If feelings were mutual, love would be a luxury we all
can afford.

The subtle touch of his lifeless body,
A coldness,
A winter walking amongst summers that are hesitant to
sit on the fire place,
If life was a mistletoe surely death has an odd way of
taking our first kiss?

A machine amongst mortals,
A definition past lovers share,
The sad reality of misunderstanding,
If insanity haunts the living would psychiatrists prescribe
dying?

The chimes of his mother echoes when his battery is
low,
The un-taught lessons his father never scriptured are
installations updated by his own analysis,
A machine amongst mortals, his tombstone will scream
for those that come to the junkyard of the abandoned.

Old Age

Done with youth,
Indulged by songs of old,
The songs whispered my love for you.
Loved you more than yesterday and less than tomorrow,
Lifetime with you is destiny fulfilled,
The love of my youth and old age.
My heart is whole with yours,
My life is meaningful with you,
My days are glazed with sunshine
And nights twinkle with your stars.
My greatest achievement,
I made you mine.

Years flew by like a bird released from bondage,
We've lived and loved,
Our eyes have seen our best of times and worst of times,
Souls have danced to every harmony of joy manifested,
Our back-breaking love making has brought us our
future.

As my breath slowly fades away from my body,
As my hair colours grey and white,
As my skin forms cracks and folds,
As my voice starts to break,
As my pace shortens,
As my torso bends,
As my experience heightens,
You are the woman I poeticised about growing old with.

I've grown to like pain,
I've fallen for you repeatedly throughout our life,
I've grown to like your smile,
I've lived for your smile from the moment I woke up the
day after we met till the day I wake up in heaven,
I've grown to like death,
Because I can't bear the thought of staying alone in this
world without you.

Old age is where our love dies.

Youth

Destiny and reality,
Happiness and sadness,
Laughter and tears,
Sunshine and moonlight,
Blue skies and dark clouds,
The songs of youth.

I met you,
Met you before the hymns from the birds met morning.
I looked at you,
Looked at you in your artistic beauty like a painter's
muse,
Every flaw so perfectly curved onto the canvas.
I looked into your eyes,
Your eyes and mine like hands finding warmth in each
other's winters.

Our youth,
Our greatest achievement in discovery,
Virgin to everything,

From a kiss to when our souls intertwine.

Our first kiss,
Felt like my thirteen reasons why to live.
Our first hug,
Felt like overcoming depression and anxiety.
Our first cuddle,
Felt like a never-ending chorus of your favourite songs.
Our first soul-bonding,
Felt like a sip from the garden of Eden's fountain of
youth,
Felt like I'm yours as much as you're mine,
Felt like the first kiss, hug, cuddle and soul-indulging
encounter.

Youth is where our hearts met.

People and Places

My Daughter

You were worth your mother's pain for nine months,
Constantly her pain vibrates through me as the way she
held my hand.
The way she held my hand,
She pushed, she squeezed and cried,
A Goddess birthing a Goddess,
I could've never been more proud of you two.

Love at first sight,
A rebirth of my heart.
I'm whole again,
Your beautiful eyes,
Transcending the poet's display of stars.

If love was life
You'd live forever.
If my strength could endure time
You'd be safe for eternity.
The greatest achievement in my whole existence is
being called,
Your father.

Josphat's Memory

Throat slit on your wedding day,
Stabbed by the woman you'd die for.
Feelings erupted by your death,
Devastation followed your passing like a thunderstorm
in winter.
A boy left to captain a sinking ship,
My Titanic carries my sanity.
Depression contaminates my oxygen,
The loss of a king in the dawn of a war.
I inherited a broken heart and a broken childhood,
Death covers the abyss in the world behind my closed
eyes,
Oil stain on my white sheets.

Cancer became you.
Caterpillar turned into butterfly.
Tears ejected from my eyes
I wept, l cried.
You lived, and you died.

Natural Beauty

Natural beauty,
Your profound birth scar,
Why?,
Why cloud yourself with 'cosmetics',
Ha! Cosmetics,
Its name screams out it's forgery,
Your authentic beauty becomes your life's myth.

The way us,
Us men,
Glance at your beauty trying to install composure.
One brief look at that melanin natural beauty,
Then doth thus give us frenzy.
A majestic frenzy,
The glare of heaven's light.

Natural beauty,
Africa's shortest supply,
Why cloud yourself with cosmetics?
Your melanin natural beauty,

Your beauty,
Maketh you a queen.

Queen Natural Beauty,
Energetic in the way you glide across the cosmos,
Alluring in the way your presence makes men tremble,
Dazzling, your beauteous self billows the earth.

What more?
What more?
What more shall my heart cry out for,
Than your natural beauty,
Your natural beauty, my African Queens!

I Met You

Hearts met in a dry summer,
Fell in love instantly.
Cold showers turned into a love bath
Truly discovered months later.
Soul torpedoed from flesh to love you forever,
That Noel, blessed was the gift of salvation,
Our kiss sparked energy like shock wave therapy,
Life complete.
Virgin Heart penetrated by the love of my life,
Happiness found its home.
I'm at peace
Pain is past
Past is oblivious to my existence.
Thank you.

Time became patient,
Slow it moved.
Bloodstream injected with love heroin,
Flew away into the mist of addiction.

Addiction to your beautiful face,
Addiction to your hazel smile,
Addiction to your make-believe travelled together,
Addiction to you.

Reality stroke,
Break-ups and make-ups cascaded from the imperfect
piece,
World cried, "Leave",
Luckily allergic to the pessimistic,
Armageddon was the choice
You and I survived.

Distance surrounded our ground like oceans
Physically distant but mentally like phrase 'heaven and
earth' inseparable.

Months passed away,
One night to prove world wrong,
You and I the greatest masterpiece
But world was right,
I, the shadow,
Became nothing more.

You danced,
You were happy on your own.
Heart sank, crushed, destroyed, obliterated,
Finally you shot me on that wet summer.
I died.
I hoped for a miracle but I saw you were happy.

Renee

Death is a continuous happiness,
A continuous happiness for the deceased.
Ren,
The limelight of my show,
The breeze under the summer sky,
The beautiful smile,
The constellation in her eyes.
Ren,
Why did you have to leave?
Why didn't I play the songs from my heart?
Was I on mute?
Countless infinities I saw us spending together,
Our future was vast like the ocean,
Our minds were intertwined like an apocalypse.
Tell me, how can I fathom your death?
Was I dead inside before we first met?
Your death turned me into a corpse.
You died without knowing,
Knowing how much your hello scratched a mile long
smile across my face.

Your sickness was saddening,
Your death was a grenade explosion on my heart.
I've always kept you close to my heart,
I saw your pain but I was too weak to help you carry it.

This is a eulogy.
I will not mourn today but tell you, tell everyone,
You were the best at being you,
You were perfect with your flaws,
You were an amazing woman, Ren,
I know heaven welcomes you home.
I won't say much today
For today till I die I will look to the heavens and remind
you of the angel you silently scream out to be.
I will be with you soon,
Your love from the other side.

Gentleman

Compassionate outcast was he
Seen by the modern world as a Nazi.
Desolate was his heart
For the world didn't heart his mind,
Or cherish his cause.
A world where love is a curse,
And being nice is weak.
Pain, anger, love, heartbreak
All in a week's work.
A world where monogamy turned to polygamy.

I, a young man aged 17
Wanting a woman with similar values,
Getting women with just intimacy values.
A good guy turned bad,
Water into wine.

All the heart longed for,
Good mental telepathy,
Growing old till we're 70,

Less arguments,
Less fighting,
A good friendship,
Now that's my interpretation of wealthy.

For I see the male opposite

She 'the great female':
A mother,
A sister,
A best friend,
A lover,
A lady of great responsibility,
As a respectable DIVINE creation.
For she is my rib
And I her body.

She needs attention,
For I have all the time there is.
She needs care,
For I have all the comfort she desires.
She needs love,
For I have all the heart to give.

But the world rejects my thought,
For I have love,
and they have lust.
For I give her a rose,
and they give her the fruit.

My body says yes but my soul says no.
My child can't journey this world,
For my hopes can never be so.

In a world where 'I love you'
Means something of the opposite spectrum,
I am here holding the values.
I the guy our grandfathers of the olden age
Called a gentleman.

Michael's Ayala

Melted plastic dripping on skin,
Crucifixion of a heathen,
Darkness painted night sky,
Gaze upon the torched purgatory in my eyes,
Razor blade wrist scar in the middle of the summer,
Death of a love martyr,
Ink to paper, memories worded together,
Melodies from within the belly of the ocean,
A sailor's call to the world.

Love, death and demise,
A circle of our relationship.
In sync with depression,
Silent tears and loud smiles.
Deep conversations and thoughtful silence.
I'm on my death bed,
Silent crowd and critic eyes analysing my last song,
I lov ... (he dies).

Her Eulogy for Sam

If Death knocks we've been betrayed by hospitality,
Our infinity cut short by human frailty,
Cancer in skin and blood have decided your fatality,
Will my prayer get answered, as being ignored in silence
is a specialty,
Especially when medicine plunged into you, made you
pain effortlessly.
The integrity of a dying man is a comfort to his loving
family.
Are you telling me,
Is dying the result of living?
But the pain in your tears makes me think death is sent
heavenly.

If time could rewind like our favourite songs,
I'd tell you that you'd be a father,
And maybe you could right your father's wrongs,
And maybe I could be a great mother,
If stars could talk, a night owl I'd become,
Sing our song as I bang your drum.

Alone I can't raise a man.
Yes, a boy you and I will have.
I'll raise your seed to be like you, Sam.
You and him, Sam, the two boys I'll forever love,
I wish heaven was a prison,
At least I'd Scofield you into my arms but it's only Jesus
that has risen,
I can't question the God we believe in,
But I guess He has a plan that I have to believe in.

Clementine

The nostalgia of youth is the side effect of ageing.
Time is a dictator that feeds you death when life gets
easier,
With her smile death lost its sting as if the stars lost their
wings,
For in her eyes they landed and the constellation that is
her soul started whistling,
To the tune of her melody I danced in my feelings.
These happy feet have never felt so much at home,
For just a strand of her hair felt like my mother's
crocheting.
The way her feet clasp the summer grass made a deep
tissue massage look like torture.
If beauty was fire then the flames did scorch her.
She warmed up my soul when my existence felt like
liquid helium,
If only reality was threaded by my grandmother,
She'd make my hello feel like a thousand reasons why
loving me wouldn't be so much of a bad thing,
She'd make us fall in love with our eyes closed, because
isn't that what true love is?

Blind to the imperfections,
Sighted to beauties our insecurities could never fathom.
We would cycle to Disney happily ever after on our
rainbow tandem.
I wish I were a magician so my abracadabra would trick
you into holding my hand,
In that heaven I'd feel as if the sun found out about the
happiness of summer.
Go to the beach with me.
These were the lyricized love-at-first-sight emotions her
smile fed me,
If only unrequited love was a fashion statement that
never came in style,
Or self-love was a diamond ring only a few tend to
receive in our generation,
If only the necklace that is depression never joined my
anxiety into a confederation.

I want to question Cupid's archery,
His aim needs training, look at this debauchery.
This is more than just a inkless page of poetry,
Because the happiness in our exchanged hellos felt like I
had just won Eden's lottery.
You are everything I hoped the love of my life would be,

In your eyes I see the imperfections that perfectly sleep
On the abyss that resides where my heart once called
home.
The fantasy of a reality that is us
Is a fiction I pray manifests like the prayers my mother
used to sing in my name.
What is existence
When breathlessness is a side effect of not being the one
that makes you smile?
What is an epiphany
When dreams are the only hospitals you can mend my
broken heart from?
Is my all inadequate to make you live by my side
Throughout the time restricted infinity we call life?
Are my sacrifices too little to quench your thirst?
I am sorry for not being the universe you wanted
When all I could give you was my world.
I guess I am overthinking since you died
Before the butterflies were able to fly out for you to
notice them.
I hope you're safe on the other side.
Goodbye Clementine.

Olivia

The heaven in your eyes is passionately alluring,
I'm powerless before your smile as my anger forgets to
frown,
My thoughts of unrequited love are beyond clothing my
soul with a thorned garment,
Still my demeanour is unstirred by these
contemplations,
For your beauty ricocheted Aphrodite's reflections,
Need I say the echoes of your hellos stifle my ability to
smell your goodbyes.
Hello Olivia,
You're the woman of my dreams,
I wish reality tricked you into loving me,
You're my happiest symphony,
An unending beat of my memories to the dreams you
were loving me,
Patiently.

Alexandra's Letter

Memories are pictures of the soul.
Our infinity is a wish only God can manifest,
Our past is filled with intoxicating passions of romance
And liberties that dazzle in happiness.
Can this now be a recurring Eden
Where reality is a conundrum only snakes tempt us to
explore?
You're the goddess my Zeus patiently thundered for,
A constellation of stars yet your beauty twinkles like a
bleeping floodlight,
Under this moonlight I poeticize my love for you,
The darkness compels me to find the immaculate solace
your warm hugs shine in my existence.
Rhyme schemes are for pyramid bricks,
My intention is to converse profoundly the
Nirvana you are to my spiritual state.
If calling you mine speaks no novelty,
I dare call you my everything.

Rest in Grace

Rest in grace my dear,
Heaven calls you home,
The lifeless tomb that holds you cannot keep you silent,
The cold touch of your skin makes me warm.
My summer,
The Hazel Grace that left me behind,
The twisted fate of reality,
If only our memories can keep my sanity.

I love you:
My cry to the heavens as I know our infinity is beyond
mortal existence.
I will die for you:
My cry in hope the devils of death listen to my prayer.
If life granted wishes we'd destroy maternities and build
graveyards.

In this eulogy,
May pain fill listeners like the whips of slave masters,
May your lightning blacken before the thunderstorms of
winter.
This life is a curse,
We learn to love before we learn to lose.

Filial Son

To my Father who art in heaven,
You lift me up from the ashes of my failures,
You command me to be righteous in this life,
And I'm more than a filial son.
I am sinner and on this path I'm still a beginner,
But with you as my armour even in losses I'm still a
winner.
For your glory is the sunrise
And even when it sets, you are the light that moons the
sky.
You fight for me when I cannot even stand up for
myself.
You shield me when the arrows of temptation are
raining on me.
You sword my hand when the glory of Heaven is the
thunder that sounds in your clouds.
Just as my dad I want to make you more than proud,
Just as my mom I want to feel your embrace,
Just as my grandma I want to feel your care,
In this life and in the after.
In this faith I gladly submit to serve on your alter.

The Death of Lucy (Lucifer)

Sharpen your blade,
Harness the pain of pain,
Vision pictures of hurt,
Drown in the emptiness of the pit of existence.

Clutch your blade,
Look death with despair,
A phantom with the makeshift of an angel,
Kiss its cheek and whisper the songs of the dying raven.

Sharpen your blade,
Surrender to the epitome of darkness,
Jump off the edge of sanity,
And make sanctuary the grave you dug in the name of
tranquillity.

Clutch your blade,
Recite the incantation of the angel's advocate,
Once trust is the ground you walk,

Grab Lucy, impale his heart,
Skewer his limbs,
Stab
till the flame is dead.

Sleep Well

Love is the eyes of a widow who stares at her wedding photo,
Hearts puzzled together like a Rubik's cube,
Emotions redden cheeks as if happiness lost the lotto.
I never thought we would stick together like the inside of a glue tube,
Slow dance with me like the last song at our favourite hilltop,
Destiny found us and our in-love insanity kept us together like the twinkling dots under the moonlight.
Falling in love with you was like listening to the Songs of Solomon,
You were a spitting image of the partner mentioned in the book of Proverbs,
In this love we shared are memories made, forgetting can never steal away.

Our eyes met and I felt the connection I had with my mother at my birth,

Our hands belonged together like the universe's tragedy
of happily ever after.
We danced to our favourite song as if the air around us
was our family in attendance at our wedding,
We shared laughters in the night and giggles in the
company of our heated bodies,
We loved like it was the air we needed to live.
Beyond the clouded skies,
The irremissible Heaven awaits for your soul.
Beyond the staggered cries,
The unsuitable call for time I wish we had more of so I
could unhesitatingly love your all.
I reminisce on the first I-love-you like the nostalgia of
our first anniversary,
I dance to the beat of your heart whenever I dream of
that unworldly hug we shared,
I mumble your name whenever I see your face on
everything else that is not you,

My mind is like a hurricane in the middle of a cave,
My heart is like an intentionally sliced wrist after my
soul hung itself,
I'm dead inside to the absence of you.

If life could've been a flower I would've built you an
orchard of flowery fruit,
If I had known death was a car ride away, our walks
would've been like a song on replay As we go in circles
like the way you go around my thoughts.
If our kiss could be kept in a time capsule I'd live in it
because I still taste the strawberry on your lips,
The way I swayed with your hips,
And everything you put in our tea because of the
enjoyment of the universal sips.
I laugh in pain because this heartache is a tremor of
despair,
In the end you died,
You lived and you died,
You loved, lived and you died.

Remember me from your love left on the other side.

Brother's Memory

Fear is reserved for the monstrosity in the mirror,
My fangs sink deep into her soul like the tiled floor in
the coldness of winter,
How could your blade pierce my heart, dear sister,
I was a victim of the Stockholm even though my soul is
a Libra,
Where is the balance?

Stuck in the confusion of certainty I had to take away
your heartbeat,
Empathetic to your terror but submissive to the call to
end your mortality.
Will our mother find comfort on my shoulder once dirt
clothes you six feet,
Will she finally speak honestly on her deception of
loving me,
As she cries in pain ghouls of the damned eat your flesh
with your vegan cutlery,
The irony of watching every calorie,

Your healthy body was unfit for heaven's glory.

Aversion is an undernourished noun of our feelings of
relation,
Eunuchism is what I wish for our sperm donor,
Dear sister, I'm a product of emotional neglect and
societal detest,
Mother favoured you more as she offered my life to
organ yours,
Reality has finally sunk in me,
My words land on deaf ears as you're no longer here
with me, because of me,
This is the story of a brother's memory.
Volume 1, 2 and 3.

Love and Pain

Prison

Am l a criminal?
Will your arms be my prison?
The wolf howls at the sight of moonlight,
You're my gothic raven in my dark times,
The andromeda's twinkle.
But you, you're like a big splash of black paint in a white
room.
Am I a criminal?
Will your arms be my prison?

I deserve your smile,
A big slaughter for a well-deserved feast,
I deserve your stare
Look at me! Like closing your eyes will be the biggest
regret of your life,
I deserve your song of happiness,
Be the last thing I hear, hymn on my death bed.
I deserve your heart,

Will I be verbally skilled and act out my love to caress
your feelings?
I ask,
Am I a criminal?
Will your arms be my prison?

Subconscious Suicide

Chronic wound on my heart,
Feelings and emotions non-existent,
Lies whispered in the comfort of darkness,
Paranoid by the weight of the casket,
Poison from the viper of love,
Death tattooed on my soul,
Flaws and Sins a perfect painting of youth.

Different arrows shot instantly,
A perfect story,
Reluctant on first chances,
Captured by demons,
With a grin they say "He enjoys bondage,"
A noose on my neck jumping off the end of the world,
Will it hold me up?.

Sinner's Prayer

If sins were scars, I'd have atopic eczema,
If my pain on earth is lost in death,
I have two wishes,
Shoot me in the heart and head,
My most infected possessions,
My eyes like waterfalls of folktales,
My migraines like war drums,
My emotional pain like recurring deaths of happiness,
How I Van-Gogh my flaws on earth.
If heaven is tranquillity,
Forgive me Father for I have sinned.

Mistletoe

Soft skin clothed you,
I feel you breathe,
I stop and freeze in the moment,
I feel your heart increase and decrease pace as I move
closer,
Twinkles in your eyes fall in sync with my dark eyes,
My emotions and feelings sky rocket as I feel your body
heat increasing in this winter.
My heart and yours are one,
They hold hands to the beat of the moment,
Swiftly lifted you up and legs tangled around my waist
like shoelaces,
Look into my eyes and listen to love incantations,
Let's intertwine our lips and tongues together and tell
each other the I-love-you's our English cannot say.
Close your eyes and vision the lifetime infinities that can
be birthed from now,
Under the mistletoe I'll make you mine.

Unknown

What amounts to my worth?
A beautiful subtle sun rise,
A slight swirl under the star lit sky,
A life time of you and l,
Beautiful possibilities sentenced to measure my worth.

Failures of men is the beginning of perfection,
Struggle relates to my past like flesh and bone,
Possibilities to flourish are inevitable,
Will life let me live till such a future is now?

Time is a song, sung by life,
Eventually lyrics will end,
Words sung are cold whispers for people to remember,
The unknown reality of tomorrow is the outcome of a
just-begun war.

Death is inevitable,
Immortality is for the ones we remember to remember,
To be forgotten is karma I would never wish on anybody,
Remember me when I'm gone.

Contemplation

Take me to my grave,
Where life ceases to exist and happiness begins,
A lifetime of sorrow followed by hell's horror,
A never ending cycle of pain and suffering.

Take me to the highest cliff,
When I jump,
The moment before my death,
Let my smile radiate upon the ashes of yesterday,
Let the loud thud as I slam onto the earth be the last
sound I'll make,
Let my angel sitting on the benchlet mourn my end.

Take me to Heaven,
Where pain transforms into relief,
A fresh cold breeze on a hot summer's day,
Where sorrow becomes happiness,

A sight of water in the middle of the Sahara,
Where my scars make me more whole than the perfect
sinner.

In the end, we answer "What's next?"

Selfish

Selfish like a winter's cold,
A blue corpse awakening in the afterlife,
The pen sunk deeply in confusion,
The paper portraits the writer's demons,
In the darkest of nights,
A sudden increase in heartbeat,
An intense emotional plug on top of an emotionally
charged volcano,
Everything else becomes non-existent.
Can one fight his demons without dying inside?
In that dark moment,
The writer, in a flash, pulled into the bottomless pit of
emptiness and despair,
The crowd cheers as it's nothing more than a story,
The writer calls out silently, it's based on reality.

Sad Love

Dark clouds parade the days,
Hot rubber covers the path,
Broken glass under the eyelids,
Knife wounds scar the back,
The world bathed in torment,
Decaying corpses fill the oxygen tank
It's hard to breathe.

Your presence,
Presence like moon in my nights.
Your worth,
Worth like a million pieces of golden crowns.
Your beauty,
Beauty ever so defined by God's right hand,
Darkest of days are brighter with your touch.

Falling in love is like falling in space.
I'll never land,

I'd kiss you like it's the first time,
Happiness means that much to me.
Drunk from each other's misery,
Overzealous on our sober state,
Death has lost its sting,
Till death do us part.

Memory Lane

Bleeding skies cover my face,
Slow silent walks on the thunderous seaside,
Memories replaying like a forgotten song,
Will you be my Rose again?

Heartbreaks are cancers of the heart,
Tears, the expression of the stage four hurt.
Slowly numbness reaches my feelings,
Will my heart be cold again?

I like you,
I adore you,
I love you,
Will I say these things again?

Memories of us?
Memories of you,
You,
Will I kiss you again?

Your smile, an ending to a fairytale,
Your eyes, the gateway to Heaven,
Your face, the highest key of a gospel song,
Will I paint your face in my dreams again?

Memories felt like I was your happiness,
The fault, was it I?
Your goodbye felt like a sigh of relief,
Will I make you feel happy again?
Will I kiss your hurt and magically make it better again?
Will I hug your whole existence and make us complete
again?

The lonely walk down memory lane ...

What is Death?

Chemistry and Philosophy,
The mixture of my love for her,
The novelty of this emotion is overwhelming,
What is death?
Death,
The cessation of life,
With her I've relived life,
Every kiss feels like the first time,
The first of many,
Fill an empty jar with water,
It's complete.
What is death?
Death,
Is not knowing love.

Apotheosis

Your eyes are shells that don't hold yolk anymore,
Yours hands are winters, did summer turn into lore?
A corpse I once called mine
Are your feelings now like a nuclear sunset?
You've taught me how to love less.
Tears that effortlessly meander down your butterscotch
cheeks lacerate my existence,
I am a moon without its howling wolf,
Our love once felt like my mother's embrace at my birth,
Now it emotes grief from the rhythm of your breath,
The breath that once filled my lungs
As our kisses felt like a 4th of July we only dreamt of.
What happened to us?
Your mother saw the youth that clothed my face,
My father poeticized young love as naive,
But even if you'd let me fall I'd have loved you like
Adam did Eve,
My words could not Monalisa my feelings,
My actions couldn't act out the fault that was in my stars,

But loving you was all my heart did,
You were never a fool to me, you were everything,
A twinkling star that lullabied my nights,
The Andromeda that made the cosmos feel small when
you shouldered my misery.

I am a broken vase that can never be mended,
My insecurities stopped me from becoming the man of
your dreams,
My hesitation stopped me from fighting for you,
I guess your mother could see right through me,
She saw the fraud I tried hard not to be,
She saw my efforts as not worthy because you were a
dandelion in the desert I called my Nirvana,
A hope I can equate to the bliss of the psalms,
I guess your love for me couldn't remedy my illness.
You are the apotheosis of the one that got away,
I want you to know,
Regret is a distant cousin I never think of when I
reminisce on us,
I guess maybe we were stuck in our own galaxies,
How repellent our love was,
Made us feel like our love in the end was unrequited.

The way you made butterflies emerge from the depths
of my soul,
The way I looked into your eyes under that February
night sky,
The way we both walked each other home repeatedly as
if tomorrow couldn't come fast enough,
The way I'd read your lips so I could say your words
back in a split second to make you think we were meant
to be,
Even though I was with her longer,
Our short time felt like a forever I'd die for with a
mythical medieval bravado,
You told me about parts of you that have never
embraced the shining of the sun,
You too have seen parts of me I denied to my
grandfather before he left for the Pearly Gates,
You've seen the tattoos that camouflage my slit wrists,
You've seen the extra tinted dark glasses that hide my
relationship with my uncle,
I was afraid of being the man I hated and I ended
becoming everything I dreaded,
You are the apotheosis of the one that got away.
Regret is a distant cousin I never think of when I
reminisce on us,

I guess maybe we were stuck in our own galaxies,
Made us feel like our love in the end was unrequited,
The way you made butterflies emerge from the depths
of my soul,
The way I looked into your eyes under that February
night sky,
The way we both walked each other home repeatedly as
if tomorrow couldn't come fast enough,
The way I'd read your lips so I could say your words
back in a split second to make you think we were meant
to be,
You suffered the worst of me,
I drained you like a cancer that stops you from eating,
A sickness that makes the stranger's dog cry at my sight,
It is such a strange thing.

My Last Letter

Black rose petals trailing to my grave,
White garments cover my darkest hour,
Lullaby of the reaper laid me to rest with a grin,
Different afterlife thoughts sunk water into sand,
The tick of time fallen from its life of rhyme,
Will Heaven offer me a home?
Will Nirvana be obtained?
Will this mere chance of my existence be worth the
sadness?
Will the beat of nothingness dance with me?
Uncertainty a gunshot wound to the head, proven very
fatal.

Cry to the memory of the unachieved,
Weep to the I-love-you's not told,
Death visits in the middle of a sente...........

Decisions

She left me shallow,
Weary of the I-put-you-first decisions,
Wrong turns made,
But for that moment
The sunrise never seemed so beautiful,
The smell of you in my sheets was comforting,
And my never-fall-asleep as I watch you sleep was not
cynical,
I put you on top, yes at the highest pinnacle,
I never understood those of old,
They whispered when I poeticised about you,
Heartbreaks makes a man a philosopher,
I'd write a thousand words on why I'd fight for you
But can never find a single way that defines my love for
you.

You took my beating heart,
Repeatedly stabbed it with your I-don't-feel-the-same-
because-they-always-leave.

First decision made wrong,
You compared me,
Compared me to wolves as I am a sheep,
I was strong enough to carry us,
Continuously fought me,
Second decision made wrong,
You saw me as a single wolf,
I am a lone pack,
Contradicting myself because maybe if I use your words
you'd understand.

Wolf-Man

A cantlet of reality floats in the abyss,
Insanity blackens the view,
The dancing light hovers above,
Taunting me to chase it,
Effortlessly I jump,
The great stretch between the glare and me cut short,
I slowly move to the silent beat and dance in sync with
the radiant light.
What enchantment is this?
Why do you feel warm?
Why do I look at you and feel like every second is the
first?
The untiring state like a painter's muse,
A serial killer's favourite weapon,
You are the art of seduction.

Enigma

The psalms surround sound the surrounding of this
morgue,
The lifeless corpses that dance in boyish vigour,
The heart that calls out his name but stuck in the lucid
sleep paralysis that is existence,
The lungs that gasp for air in the water that baptised the
contritioned patrons,
The undeserving masses that skull the soil but divine
forgiveness can save them all,
Unimaginable power that makes canvas of nothing and
creation a simple shallow breath,
In the night sky a twinkle appears in the interstellar I
hope where he is,
A kingdom even the Romans prostrated for,
A sonnet even Shakespeare can never romanticise
about,
A love a mother cannot conjure for her dying son,
A joy even mysticism cannot philosophise,
Who am I in the break of dawn?
Who am I in the midst of salvation?
A mere wondering sheep yearning for my master.

The voice that thundered and let sky lit up with the sun,
The voice that showered and let rain flood the oceans,
The voice that breathed into clay and let man govern his
creation,
An enigma is he as I cry for his intellect,
An enigma is he as he crafted with us rooting on its
stem,
An enigma is he as he loved my flaws when I cannot
even love myself.
The security that brings scrutiny to my insecurities,
The purity that proudly identifies with me.

I shed tears at the thought of your Son,
The suffering servant Isaiah prophesised,
The Son that died so that I may find salvation,
Elevated on the cross he poeticized to the heavens
Eli Eli Lama Sabachthani,
For in his pain as the Holy Lamb he accepted his pain,
For in his pain as the Holy Lamb I was worth dying for,
As I call to all the Christian soldiers,
Hear your Lord's command and march till Heaven's gate
is on the other side of our awakening eyes.

Two Spectrums of Love

A fiend, the boy in the disfigured mirror,
His demeanour, a hellhound from the belly of the beast,
Raised in the south but descended from the east,
Deceased.
His soul in the eyes of the living,
Succubus, the woman in his dreams the sexual pleasures
she's filling,
And Beelzebub, on his soul his nibbling,
Injections of ice for the feelings his numbing,
Now prepare for the second coming.

Angela, the pretty nun from the times of no religion,
Incubus in her dreams is the boy she's yet to be loving,
Cumming, is all she thinks about as he's overly whelming
her flowering, that's empowering,
Character, a definition her beyond heavenly existence
can encompass,
Which of us,

Sings Angela as she waits for Prince Dominic to catch
her chorus,
Like Horus, his black wings, the moon and the sun his
eyes discovers,
A flawless humanoid on the land of the graves,
How brave is Angela as she throws away distance,
Don't miss it,
She whispers as her heart finds solace in Dominic's
presence ,
The essence,
Of two spectrums birthed in the same existence,
Who is it?
The heathen priest calls to those in attendance,
To deny these two of an infinite happiness,
In the midst of the countless I-love-you's,
Death stands up and shouts,
Here lies,
The boy and the girl that once were.

Her Justice

Statistics show the gender's misconduct,
Failure to provide security brings insecurity,
We claim to have changed the world but not ourselves
what is the helpline contact?
Details of sadistic assaults that arts the painting of
superior inferiority,
This is a song of an eagle that lost her ability to fly.

You and I shall live longer than her lifeless living body,
Feeling sorry is inadequacy to the actions needed to be
taken,
Awaken from the slumber and stop painting your
timeline holy,
Holly was an ambitious candidate of success till she
became a victim of the numbness,
Congratulations now she loves less,
The song is a hurricane of emotions trying to write in
white ink on grey tiles,
Sit down let me open the dark files.

On the road down Confidence Lane,
Lurking deeply in the shadows of toxic masculinity,
Natas slithered to inflict pain,
Holly in sight, Natas cried out in levity,
"Hey, miss, can my shivering body be warmer with yours?"
"Can my girth fill your holes?"

Natas grinned as she started pacing,
His bravado choked her anxiety and for the gods' grace she was patiently waiting,
A saviour was a 5 inch knife her anxiety pushed her to forget,
Detect the detest before you're quick to pass the test.

Natas like a wolf pouncing on its prey jumped on her effortlessly,
Pinned to the ground she cried out loud breathlessly,
Impatiently he smacked her repeatedly,
The second cousin of anxiety is trauma.
She suffered badly,
Muted by the fists Natass' mother once kissed at birth,
How could this man stand brave in the name of inflicting hurt?

He grazed tongue on her neck as she felt ready for
death,
Disgusted she cried silently as he ripped her dress
proudly,
Repeatedly he had his way into her womanhood forcibly,
Possibly if this nightmare could be vaporized she would
have forgotten her whole existence.

Listen,
A poet once said gods cry at night,
And still nobody bothered to check my plight,
If rape is an equation then its answer is the square root
of men,
Calculate the calculations and beware of
misinformation,
If you're threatened by the movement then you're part
of the problem,
Solvents make solutions,
You and I brother should be included,
Let's fight for our women.

Eclipse

You and I were materials of opposing compounds,
I, a vase dropped repeatedly till the past I tried to
cremate became whole with the air,
You, a fantasmic being even the coding Da Vinci
couldn't unlock with his mysticism,
Your beauty a calculus equation my eyes calculates with
the help of my beating heart,
Your eyes a harpoon that thrusts deeply into my soul
whenever our eyes collide,
Your hands feel like my mother's touch when the
midwife placed me on her palms,
Your kiss is poetry that romanticises war as I battle the
effortless urge to fall for you religiously,
You are the sun that evaporates my pain,
I am the moon, I hope I make your wolf howl at night,
Let us eclipse again.

Lost but Found

What is life's meaning?
A gaze upon a horizon of straightened possibilities,
What do you believe in?
A question that nudes your insecurities,
Again my soul asks what is life's meaning?

Conflictions are tumours of the mind,
Lost but found is my mantra as my head makes beats
with the white painted wall,
The answer to the existential crisis is harder to admit
than it is easy to find,
She is mine, the screams I hear when men's search for
meaning turns twin religions into a brawl,
Crawl, into the epitome of emptiness,
Love experienced teaches to love less,
The answer my pastor gave me doesn't make sense,
Believe and rewards of completion shall fill your soul,
Does a happy dream make reality more miserable?

In the chasm riddled on my chest,
A star beyond the sun shines in desire,
Cast the search in the fire and pass the test,
Desires are addictions of imagination,
Rationality leads to conclusions but never the answers.

I Swear

Who is the examiner of reality,
Who is the philosopher that made us learn lessons
before we found the answers in our backyards,
From maternity we jump into the mortuary,
Does the coldness stop the decay or does the midwife
prolong it?

Who is the artist that painted the sky?
Does her impressionist brush paint her reflection for us
to ponder?
Who watered the oceans?
Does he cry when we suffer our self-inflicted karmic
misery?
Who is the poet that uttered the word faith?
Does she hope he will change when materialism shows
its value?
Who is the sword's master that cut the grass and left the
trees to tower over our double lives?

Do you see the obstruction on the straight line?
Do you like the taste of vinegar when the kiss is under
the grape vine?
Do you dance to the beat of your heart or it never skips
often enough?
Do you hug your kids every day and tell the emotional
creditors that you do not believe in love,
It is tough, maybe a little rough,
Privately decaying and publicly blooming with your
reversed frown,
Before the King of the universe let us take both knees,
If death is tomorrow then to heaven take me please,
The collection of books is a philosophy I'm learning to
need,
By your crown show mercy to me as I am in need.

I swear upon the debtors of my anxiety,
I swear upon the fraudsters of my morality,
I swear upon the looters of my honesty,
And the I swear upon the givers of my faced cruelty,
If lessons are learnt from your teachings then let death
be an oath I take in this poetry.